Unwritten Letters

Unwritten Letters

Aarti Bhardwaj

To Mom and Her Belief

Acknowledgements

As I present this collection of poetry, my heart overflows with gratitude. This journey, from the first verse to the last, has been one of deep introspection, discovery, and growth. It would not have been possible without the unwavering support and encouragement of many wonderful people.

A special shout-out to my dear friend Abhishek Singh, who endured countless threats and late-night wake-up calls just to read drafts and provide feedback at the earliest. He has been my consistent reader, never complaining about the length of the content. I owe a great thank you to Yasmeen Khan, who has been a consistent believer in me and always motivated me and held her faith high in me when I was feeling not so sure about completing the project. Also, my friend Shikha Singh who always said that she is not big at reading but she would like me to narrate her what I write. That is the most beautiful thing about her contribution.

To Mr. Ashok Mukherjee, whose wisdom and guidance illuminated the importance of publishing this collection, Col Bhawani Singh Nirwan, whose unwavering support has been a beacon of light on this path—thank you both immensely.

I also extend my heartfelt thanks to all my friends Jyotsna Chopra, Sutapa Chakravarty, Saakshi Murdia, Indrani Biswas, who took the time to read my drafts and offer invaluable feedback. Your motivation has been a true source of inspiration.

To my mother—Tara Bhardwaj, your encouragement and belief in me never wavered. Your faith, strength and love as it reflects in me have inspired countless lines in this collection. Your belief in me has been the wellspring of my inspiration.

And to you, the reader, who now holds the essence of my spirit in your hands—thank you for embarking on this journey with me. May these writings resonate with you as deeply as they have with me.

With deepest appreciation, **Aarti Bhardwaj**

CONTENTS

SOLITUDE

Holding on to the breath
        That is craving to pass by,
Lurking in the moment
That threatens to leave thy,
Craving for the beat that heart would defy,
Sensing my love with the most envious cry.

Oh ! how invincible is the feeling
That makes me die,
Living in the ocean with a drop of cry.

Loving you was not easy, but leaving you is,

How many breaths I had to skip,
With how many beats I had a tiff.

Longing for the feeling as long as I live,
Where the heart would come back to me
And spell bliss.

RAINDROPS

I remember the day
    when our eyes met,
And I remember all that too,
When your lips quivered,
And deceived you.

Remember, my love,
You will sense the caress
Of that rain,
Reminiscing of when you felt me,
With those tiny droplets,
Streaming down your face,
Kissing and enveloping you.

When I reflect on that moment,
I wish
I were there with you.

DRIFT

Why do I feel adrift today,
　　　Lost in thoughts that won't go away?

Is it bècause you wander astray,
Leaving me alone once again to sway?

Are you waking up with someone new,
Leaving me to wonder what to do.

My heart aches with every passing view,
As I yearn for the love that once was true.

REMEMBER

When all is forgotten,
Remember to come to me,
To embrace love again,
Like sunshine glistening over streams.

When all is forgotten,
Remember to dance on a breeze,
Descend into the dusty sapphire,
In the shadows of Amethyst.

When all is forgotten,
Remember to soar above the skies,
Perch on the highest bough
And never lose sight of the rainbow.

When all is forgotten,
Remember to tread on the heavens,
Recline in meadows lush green,
Gaze at the stars and return their twinkling.

When all is forgotten
Remember to visit me in dreams
Gently touching once more,
Reigniting souls as you breathe,
Together, forevermore.

Lost in this eternal moment,
A Love, Long ago, we lived,
Remember my Love, Remember.

Let memories,
Guide us back to each other's light.
As we walk in heavens,
Like constellations bright.

MOMENTS

How can I forget
        the thirst of that moment
When I poured to touch you !!

How am I supposed to pray
for a moment with you,
When I held my breath for a lifetime,

To breathe in a moment with you !!

TRANCE

Tender promises turn into twilight,
Your golden locks fade into dawn,
I dream of warm summers,
As dew drops from my eyes,
Waiting for spring to arrive,
And make dreams fly.

Come close to me and whisper a lie.

As your face bathes in moonlight,
I linger on as I dispel the night,
I dream of fragrant springs,
As you kiss me sunshine,
And dark blue nights
Watch the time fly by.

Come close to me and whisper a lie.

In the stillness, I behold your gentle sigh
You wrap me in a warm embrace divine
Beneath the auburn sky.

I dream of the rivers,
And memories softly rise,
They fade to mist,
As I drown in tides.

Lost in the whispers of forgotten rhymes,
Come close to me and whisper a lie.

Let's dance upon the water,
Like stars in the night sky,
Come close to me and
Haunt me through blue nights.

Let the rivers carry my burning,
Through the darkness, out of sight,

Come close to me and
Make me miss you all night.

7

ARRIVAL

I walked in a dream and followed upstream
  The way above the rainbows
And the curve beyond the world's end.
I tiptoed on the violet edge
And lurked there for a moment.
Eternity scattered at the end of the view,
Lifetimes ahead and lifetimes through.
My legs trembled on a hint of return
I reminisced and paused for a moment
I craved to become part of that view.
I closed my eyes and I thought of home
All I could see was me lying alone
Engulfed with sorrow and tears unbound,
Of my dear ones and those who were my own.

I started a journey leaving all alone
And I arrived before I was gone.

IT'S SO

Do you think it's time to reach the skies
        And that's another season bide,
Then it's so my love.

When you smile all bright and shy
And see the heaven came to lights
Then it's you, my love.

When you think of taking my hand
And ride along with me, my friend
It's going to be love.

It'll be lasting as the moon and tides
And forever live as you desire,
Pure and true, that we share
And nothing can ever break
This bond we bear.
It's got to be love.

TRAVELS

Hand me your dreams
    Watch them bloom and thrive,
Treasured in realms of
My heart and my being,
I'll carry them till I die.

Oceans and trees, starlings and lilies
Weeping willows and cheers,
All that is pink, all that is blue
Painting the canvas of our years.

Holding your hand I can travel to the land
Where skies meet earth and bleed,
Flying on the fears and grounding the seers
We'll walk on clouds till we gleam.

Faith and belief, like emerald leaves,
Simmering in pots of tears,
All that is far all that is gone
All you thought lost is here.

Climb with me on a ray over stream
I'll show you the dawn, my dear,
Riding the winds across distant seas
We'll find the way, it's near.

Mountains and freeze,
Amaranthine dreams,
Rainbows beneath the fears,

All that's bathed in Sun
All that's kissed by the Moon
All that you've dreamed is here.

RUSH

My eyes are drizzly
And my heart is aflame,
My breath was struggling
Also ceased in vain.

I drowned and
Started trickling somewhere,
A teardrop that welled
And turned into a torrent from nowhere.

Burning every desire that was
Inflamed and extinguished,
The ocean of breath turned into
Ash and smoke from nowhere.

I found you dear the moment
I was buried, in love,

I wonder why I waited alive
And what I was living for.

VISION

I f I were to love you
       How could I possibly do that,
   It would mean floating on your arms
   While you slumber beside me,
   And craving for your touch,
   Whilst you were lingering around me,
   It's the press of my heart against yours
   When your slender fingers
   Are wandering on my shores.
   It's the nibble I feel on my ears
   And the breath I draw while rushing near,
   It's the peace on my face reflecting my tears,
   When you hold me close, so close, my dear.
   Yes, it's the flame that rises
   From rubbing of the souls,
   And yes it's the pain that sizes
   The churning all along.

   I am here with the song,
   You sang,
   While you were gone,

I was here with your arms around
When you embraced me long.

I was here when it happened
And, when it did not,
I am here with the morn
That returns every dawn.

I am here with you dear
To stay forever long.

And if I were to love you
You wouldn't be gone.

INTOXICATION

Reminiscing the memories besprinkled,
I keep returning to your reflection,

You,
Pressing your lips,
Against my hands
Once more,
And with love,
Tenderly kissing my wrists,
You held me close,
To your heart
Delicately,
And enthralled me with
Your gentle embrace.

How scanty
Were those
Fragrant and
Intoxicated evenings !!

MEMORIES

I sat under a tree
    Savoring the memories
They are endless,
Every time I think of them
They allure me to their land.

A fresh trickle from the rain
Washes down like your warm embrace
Spinning desires to hold hands
And the tremors that follow without end.

A thing as simple as Heather
May take its place on virgin grounds,
When touch as divine as yours
Makes its way to shovel what's drowned.

PAIN

It dwells in the hearts and the missing parts
Of the life we cradled and bore thy joy,
Some traversed near and some left shy.
In the chilly nights,
I spent apart and distant
Where howling of feelings and
Sorcery of wishes was rampant,
Echoes of thoughts fell upon me
When I negotiated their word against me.

Scattering spoils and decaying the toils
Extinguishing every illuminated joy,
My face covered in the blood of my ties
And what not should be told of those lies.

Thoughts slithering in my bed,
Stinging every inch of life, I thought I had.
Banished by love I thought I would stay,
Blistering my soul along the way.

Witches of sorrow were eyeing prey,
And I became the one who came into their way.
With the bemoaning of wishes drowned,
My heart is saddled with thorns in crown.

I let my heart bleed and died in vain
If only I knew it was just Pain!

HOME

The feeling so unraveling,
    A caress that curves the ocean within.
The fluttering of the nerves ridging in
Feverish breaths rising to meet the fount,
Lips pining with fervor for
A touch that taunts.

The glistening of dreams
Dancing in the waking eyes,
The touch so heavenly that
Makes me quiver and shy.

The ambrosial murmurings of softer dawns,
Whispering of souls and melting of morns,
Aromatic embraces embroidering the gaps between,
Meandering the gasping shallows upstream.

How am I to sketch what I long for,
How am I to subscribe to,
What is called for ?

Returning of dawns
After such meetings and
Ailing for touch that inflames
Cold heart to beating.

And I live yet another day for,
Oh ! This heavenly feeling !

DREAMS

T he world is a beautiful place
      To go adrift in,
Inviting you to leave your soul behind,
It makes you see from
Its bewitching lies.

Every day we get a chance,
To save ourselves from
the world's trickery,
Dreams are the passage to that land,
Where life can make no mockery.

Dreams, are the light from the universe
That awakens our souls,
They are the messengers of our
Buried desires in the daylight,
The reflections of ourselves,
Unfurled and pristine.

Dream we must for if we don't,
We will trade our dripping souls,
Lost, in a world's seductive charade.

Our real self takes refuge in dreams
For we are fearful beings.
Daylight might cause our faith to dilute
We seek solace in shadows of solitude.

Dreams don't require the practical fleet
What truth in daylight might defeat.

We wander in the garden
Of thoughts lush green,
While also unfolding
The creature within.

Dream we must for if we don't,
We might lose the stranger
We long to embrace.

In the times of deepest emotions,
And times of unfathomed illusions,
Mystery of hearts makes life surreal,
Dreams become the bridge to sense it for real.

Reality stings even with the tail,
And every time we don't understand,

We fail.

Dream we must for if we don't
Dark of despair might
Make its way home.

Light makes way as the dark falls in
Glittering like dreams and wishes burning.
Bathed in white and covered with scars.
Paths dissolve as moonlight wash.

Dreams whispers of angel
And of the devil,
For dreams are noble
And dreams are evil.

Dream we must for if we don't,
We will sign a way
One must never move to.

Dreaming of the past doesn't make it better,
Dreaming of the future doesn't light its feather,
Dreams of the could have's, don't seem to belong,
When dreams of the would have's,
Become weary and prolonged.

Dreams become a burden that we carry on,
With the departures of dear ones,
And the gloomy love songs.

Dream of the hearts that,
Lovers desire to bloom,

And of the good bye's,
Which makes life even truer.

Dream you must, for if you don't,
Melancholy drives your future
With a dash of Blue.

Dream you must,
For they are woven from starlight,
They knit our souls, as they wonder,
In beautiful whispers, quietly they slumber,
Let dreams be your guide,
In their depths, our essence confides,
Give them a chance to breathe tonight.
Close your eyes and surrender to sleep,
From dream's embrace, a brighter dawn do leap.

THAT'S LIFE

Dawn turns to rust as the day ends its life
Stars also burst in their never-ending bright
Holding the blacks till it turns to white
Life takes its journey in such eternal flights.

Days go by with dripping of the hours
Years go by when memory devours
Life settles against little showers
More the rains less the hours.

Racing to finish what life had start
Thinking about days and times we retort
Leaving ourselves behind in parts,
For the sake of time, we never got.

Let's make moments drip from the days
Let's make days longer than stays
Let's live this life as it sprouts
Holding the flame before it burns out.

Let's make it easier to make life count
By taking every breath we discount
Let's dream and wake up the day
Let's scream and live our way.

Let the drenching sun light up the rain
And mark doors close that betray,
A day is dead when it's not lived,
A ray is set when it's not at your feet.

Build the doors and pave your way
For new light is shining o'er making hay,
As the Sun rises in the next flight
Start this life with utmost delight.

18

ASH AND CLOUDS

You've been leaping
From the windows to the
rivers Down in the night,

And watching smoke rising from the
Bodies burning inside,

You wish to stay but take a turn,
Tell me why,

You can't help it but to burn,
Tell me why,

You wish to stay forever,
And you just can't say goodbye.

Kisses in the forest and
They are hidden in the graves of cry,
Lovers wrapped in their arms and
It's difficult to say die,

You have been missing forever,
Tell me why,

This heart beats no longer,
Tell me why,

You have been watching me forever,
And you just can't say goodbye.

When you're alone, I'll be with you,
When you are through, I'll be there too.

And these are
My last words to you !

19

A NEW DAY

Winter mornings and dew drops falling
        Inviting cheer as life is calling,
Moon is chasing the Sun,
As it drips through the dew,
For Dawn is set and a year is new.

Eyes have filled up with
The essence of dreams
Waiting to nurture life
As morning kicks in.

May the mornings of the new year be blessed,
and the days brighter and fresh,
May we achieve all we long,
"May we become what this year belongs".

20

LONGING

If I could tell by the
        Look of your eyes
I'd say that
I found the gateway
To my conscience
In your eyes.

If I were to taste
The warmth of your lips
I'd say I found the
Ever-flowing sap of life to
Quench my thirst forever.

If I could forever
Trace your contours
Just to be reminded
Of the traverse
That belongs to me.

If I were to feel you
Amidst the breaths,
I'd whisper I found the spark
That ignites my soul
To and fro,
As it travels.

21

SECRETS

Into the deepest shallows of heart
   Hides the creature,
Threatening to take away the secrets,
I have been keeping from the world.

It coils in the dark of my dysphoria,
It lives on your memory, while it devours me
Its life exceeds mine, as it destroys me.

It lurks in the deepest of my desires,
Stirs in the embrace when our bones are afire,
As I inhale your fading scent,
It dissolves my walls from within.

The luminance of which is so high,
It covers shadows and steal the coming night,
And it pulses within, the secrets
I cannot hide.

I waited for you to leave
Till I hear your breath no more,
And not even a sound of murmur,
When you took piece of my soul and a lot more.

I held the moment close,
A fragile ember's glow,
But with your leaving,
Only ashes flow.

Languishing in the pain of parting,
I will sleep alone,
Tormenting in the middle of the night,
The silence lives on.

In the recesses of my heart,
I drowned it forever,
It stayed throbbing,
Like a pulse,
Without a heart,
And it stayed as life,
With soul pulled apart.

I saw your reflection in a trance,
With you gone that night,
And relinquished my heartbeat,
To dark, to meet your light.

And the creature, unleashed,
Awakens to claim its prize.

22

HOLDING ON

Savoring memories of the past,
I pause the rush of life to make it last.

My desires, my essence,
my senses and my heartbeat,
Bound eternally to fly and sing.

To dance in the moon and cry for my sins,
Grasping onto what's left to live
Clutch my love to soothe the sting,
Immersing myself in the depths of my being,
to embosom..

Oh ! this profound feeling !!

A BIRTHDAY WISH

Birthdays are the days from above
    When life is full of cheer and glow
Beneath the wings of charming sight
Life starts turning for a new flight
The journey that takes you far in the sky
Taking the travels of your lifetime
On your day, I wish the same,
Put your wings on and take the game
I know you must win,
you must fill in the dates
With all the love eternally
Poured in to date.
I know you will win,
and

On this day
"I Gift You a Wing"

* * *

<u>FOR PARENTS</u>

The birth of a baby is a blessing from above
When angels guard the ways and stars take a bow
Being a parent is a gift of God
When most awaited dreams
Wake up in the arms below.
For a child is a miracle that changes hearts,
And they pave the way for a rather brighter start,
May your miracle bind you and hold,
For long loving life is yet to unfold.

* * *

<u>FOR CHILD</u>

Birthdays are those heavenly days from above
When Mom labored love and Daddy hold on,
The birth of an angel became their destiny
When You "sweetheart" took
the shape of their eternity.
May your life always be full of cheer and glow
May you make Mommy and Daddy
proud as you grow,
May the love bestowed upon you wherever you go,
May you sculpt new worlds
for everything you want to do.

24

CONVERSATIONS

No more words to share,
　　No message left to spare.
Our paths have intertwined,
No more roads to find.

Together we stood,
The whole world was in our view.
But you chose to depart,
Leaving behind a heavy heart.

Now I stand alone,
In the end, all on my own.
The memories we shared,
Are all that's left to be cared for.

Oh, how I longed to see,
The future that could be.

But now I must accept,
That our story is incomplete.

25

LOST

Souls igniting every desire aflame,
Shuddering with every breath,
A name on my lips,
A whispered refrain.

Dreams are fragrant, wild and free,
Passion waiting to be claimed,
Like raindrops on this virgin land,
untouched by pain, unashamed.

Lost, in this moment
You and I,
A symphony
Forever to remain.

REVERIE

In the hush of quietude,
    Where words retreat,
Silence unfurls its
Enigmatic mystery,
A canvas woven of introspection,
Each thread a whisper,
A question, a mystery.

In this stillness,
Emotions find their sanctuary,
An unspoken ache,
A joy too fragile to say,
Gathered on morning petals
Like dewdrops,
Awaiting the dawn
When language will reclaim.

Stars conversing in
Cosmic dialects,
Their luminous syllables
Painting the night,

And the moon,
A silver oracle,
Guards secrets,
Its craters etching
Tales of forgotten light.

Hushed embraces,
Bridges our heartbeats,
Longing surrenders,
With a gentle flow.
It cradles dreams,
Like boats of paper frail,
Travel to horizons unseen,
On whispers they sail.

And perhaps,
Within this quietude's embrace,
We discover truths
That eludes the scene,
For sometimes,
The most profound revelations,
Reside not in words,
But in the spaces between.

27

INSCRIPTIONS

Will I forget you?
      Difficult it is.
Will I remember you?
Hard to know!
What will happen in the end?
It depends on you.
Are we going to meet again?
All I know is, that I'll spend
My life and after without you.
Shall I be worried?
If you hold on to me!
How can I find you?
Bring flowers for me.

Can I be with you?

Forever Love,
But not so soon!

REST

This is the place where I would lie,
    A place where the sun kisses the shore,
Where life is blurred and past,
And the thoughts never die.

This is where the lavender will grow,
And take my scent to the sky,
I'll nourish it with my passing,
And the grass here will never turn dry.

This is where lovers will find solace,
And get their head straight,
Where no one will judge them,
And I will lend an ear to their endless unrest.

This is where seas of emotions will flow astray,
As the rock beneath them remains at bay,
They will rise high and never recede,
As I will be the sparkling tide guiding the cascade.

This is the place where I tell you,
I have always loved you true,
Feel the fragrance of the lavender,
You will find it growing more blue.

This is where, if you shed any tears,
They will find their way through,
To the shrine in my soul
And return as a shower of rain to you.

And when I die,
I will rest my soul here,
And let my body burn,
So whenever you are cold,
I will give my warmth to you.

29

LOST & FOUND

My heart was troubled
For someone
Until you appeared,
Like a guiding Sun,
Moments were entangled,
Like threads of loom,
And the sky, once maroon,
Now brightened the room.

The shadows deepened,
Mirroring my grief,
I felt myself drowning,
Seeking some relief,
Yearning to grasp that
Fleeting moment's embrace,
Yet the wait grew so long,
It slipped without a trace.

Weaving dreams
In the fabric of time,
Life enfolds,

An intricate rhyme.
Desperately wandering,
Seeking what I'd lost
Unaware of whom I await,
And at what cost.

Whose dream am I but the fragment of,
Whose sky I am tucked away!

Tormented again by the desires,
Lost in life's race,

I yearn for someone
While chasing life's pace.

30

COLD

I slept with the window open
    Allowing the blizzard in,
While I patiently awaited your return.

I was frozen to death,
By your disdain too.

When you come back,
Bring some warmth, my dear,
Heal the rift too.

So that the ice thaws,
And feelings merge through.

You know it well,
That you bring bliss,
With tears dwelling through.

Every time you say goodbye,
You shatter my heart anew.

JOURNEYS

L ost and stranded
        On the road to eternity,
The path you took
Never led to me.

I am troubled
To have lost you,
On a journey
That wasn't mine,
But was meant to be.

NATURE

A winding road through fields of gold
    A tale longing to be told,
The sun-kissed path, the whispering breeze
Through woods, under ancient trees.

Adventure calls from distant lands,
In the depths of nature, where secrets stand,
Footsteps echo on the rugged ground,
Unraveling mysteries that abound.

The world unfolds in vibrant array,
Every step unveils a new display,
From mountaintops to valleys deep,
The journey teaches our souls to keep.

As twilight falls, we pause to reflect
The wonders witnessed, the moments perfect,
The journey enriches, our hearts aglow
For in the wanderings, our spirits grow.

So let's embrace the winding road,
The story waiting to unfold,
For in the journey, we find our way
And in each step, is a brand-new day.

SOUL

Wounded are the breaths
        By the longing,
My heart must confess
Perhaps.

A piercing through the heart
Is beyond forbearance,
A memory dwells here
Perhaps.

Beatings embracing my heart
Every moment,
Released suddenly,

I found you
Perhaps.

HEADSTONE

Whispers from the past and love profound,
Words echo, without a sound.
Upon the stone or a page,
They hold the essence of a bygone age.

Carved with care, each letter precise,
Inscribed in hearts, a lasting vice.
Whispers of wisdom, stories untold,
Legacies written in Grey and bold.

Through the hands of time, memories endure,
Inscriptions speak of love and loss.
Every flashback walks a course,
A tender reminder, its a bridge to cross.

Precious words etched deep within,
Touching our souls, where stories begin.
The words holds power to ignite
Endless love and endless light.

For all this would a single stone suffice !!

35

WHISPERS FROM BEYOND

I am the truth,
   Untouched by the tangled web
Of deceit you've woven.

And I shall persist,
As the unwavering belief,
Even when falsehoods
Envelop your world.

In the quiet of shadows,
I lurked and observed,
Each footfall etched in memory,
Every thread of choice woven
Into the fabric of your being.

The eons passed, and still,
I waited—patient, unyielding.
I've stood in silent vigil,
Since the moment of your dawn,
Yearning for the time,
When destiny would decree,

You'd awaken to my presence,
And forever merge with me.

The moment, when
My arms would enfold you,
And our souls interlace,
And you would recognize me,
For what I am : your own truth,
Long sought and now revealed.

And now, as stars bear witness,
To the truth we've always known,

In my embrace,
You're finally home.

36

LASTING FLAME

In the depth of memories, my heart unfolds,
    As it fathoms a tale untold.
A flame once bright, now flickering low
Yet the embers of passion, refuse to let go.

A chance encounter, a sultry glance
Unexpected and rare, has woven a snare.
Ashes resurrect, and spark takes flight,
As our eyes meet, igniting besotted light.

Whispers of yesteryears reverberate,
And echoes of laughter once lost are awake.
We tread the familiar paths with newfound grace
Rekindling a love with eternal embrace.

Hearts may have changed, but scars remain
Like memories etched in the mirror of pain.
With relentless storms upon the shore,
Embracing fiercely what was lost to views.

In the ebb and flow of love's tide,
We embrace fleeting whispers that bide.
Navigating winding paths of highs
A fabric woven, where love still survives.

As fate intertwines our paths once more,
I feel the familiar tides of love's shore.
A whispered melody, a tender touch
Memories of connection that meant so much.

In the depths of the past, memories ignite
Flames rekindled, burning oh ! so bright.
Lost love lingers like a haunting song,
A tale unfinished, righting the wrongs.

Love's journey, hearts may change,
Lost it may be, its essence remains.
Revisiting, a bittersweet space,
Love's a flame that flickers,
But its warmth remains.

WAIT

I wait for you in every dawn
   And every starry night,
I long for you in every breath
And every ray of light.

I wait for you to come to me
And fill my heart with bliss,
I long for you to hold me close
And seal it with a kiss.

I wait for you with hope and faith
And never lose my trust,
I long for you with all my soul
And never quench my thirst.

I wait for you, my dearest love
And always will, I swear;
I long for you, my only one
And always will, I care.

38

PHOENIX HEART

Whispers of ghosts from the past, creep,
Weaving through the corridors of time,
A calling from love's memory perhaps,
Turning fragments of haunting moments alive.

In the recesses of my mind, they resonate,
The laughter, the touch, the tender embrace,
A faint perfume weaving time and space,
Like a cherished melody entangled in its pace.

With simmering emotions and lessons learnt,
Time drifted away with steam, leaving me burnt.
The ache of "what was" and "what could have been",
Left haunting "what if", like a forgotten dream.

With fragile wings of old feelings returning,
I bid farewell to the echoes gone by,
With reflection, I embraced a new dawn,
And a wiser heart appeared, like a colorful sky.

Unbowed by memories' crushing weight,
Love emerged, as a bright whetted blade,
Cleaving through every lingering woe,
From soul's cold ashes and love's desperate desire,
A phoenix I rise, my love, with wings of fire.

A mosaic of memories,
Where the heart intertwines,
In a sun-drenched sky,
With love reborn, I fly.

39

BLISS

Quietude of a moonlit night
    Hearts taking flight.
A gentle sway,
A Sweet romance.

Feather's touch,
Magical grace.
A soft caress,
A fleeting embrace.

A whispered vow,
Love unfold,
Flames ignite,
Passions stir.

A fervent and fiery light,
Burning touch.
Ink of lust,
Smoldering embers.

Love pursuing,

A poet's quill,
An ecstasy.
Ardor brewing,
Unleashing storm.

From tender,
To the wild.
Sweet nectar,
Steamy fire,
A memory held,
A Promise kept.

Tempest's grip,
Forbidden sip.
A lovers' steal,
Each one unique.

Raging tide,
A deep desire.
A lover's high,
Setting souls ablaze.

Hearts on fire,
Bridging of hearts.
A secret kept,
A stolen breath,
And a pact.
Essence of life,
Whispers in woods,
Forbidden wine,
Downpour.

Waves on a shore,
Fueling flame,
Thriving of souls,
Stolen hearts,
Life's intricate parts.

Petals unfurling,
Intoxicating,
Salt and Sweet.
A sacred space,
World's fade.

Time Stands still,
Love's sweet thrill,
The unspoken,
Makes heart and
Soul speak,
In a fleeting moment
Makes your
Life complete.

A poet's ink,
Ballad of love
A verse complete,
A sonnet, a melody,
A love's tale, wrought every time

So is the **KISS** !!

RHYTHM ON WIND

A secret brushed
     On the breeze,
Lighter than a falling leaf,
A gentle nudge,
A hidden key,
Unlocking joy,
You can't quite see,
A rustling whispered,
Gently,
A mystery,
The heart will keep.

Dear friend,
A rhythm on wind.

FROM THE ABYSS, I SPEAK

In the shadowed halls of eternity,
    Where stars and galaxies travel,
I, stand sentinel.

I remember when
Life was a whisper,
Your first breath, fragile as spark.

Your lips first quivered and
Blossomed like petals.
You danced—
Oh, how you danced!
In gardens of laughter carefree,
Under sun-kissed skies,

Your hearts,
Lanterns of hope
- ever shimmering,
I was there in the
Reflection of those
Joys and murmurings.

But then came tears,
- the taste of salt
Loss, like a storm,
Swept through your veins.
You, clutched your memories,
Fragile as silk,

I was the Cerulean dusk
Watching grief exhale.

At the bedsides,
I stood—silent witness.
Your breaths - flickering,
Whispered secrets to me.

I am the keeper of treasures,
I was there in confession
Of your untold stories.

There were some souls,
Departed with
Stories half-written.
Their hearts,
Still yearning to speak.
I touched their brows cold,
Kissed their eyelids close.

I was there as
The ink on the pages
Of their unwritten history.

In quiet rooms,
Some hands clasped,
Heads surrendered,
Their eyes—
Windows to infinity —
Closed in defeat.
I cradled their souls,
Like fragile sparrows.
And they soared above the veil.

I was there in the palms
When prayers whispered silently.

But listen!
In the spaces between,
Your laughter lingers,
- like an echo.
Life, a fleeting waltz,
Leaves footprints.

And I am,
But a dance partner.
The silent witness
To your every heartbeat.

So fear me not, dear,
As I am the
Weaver of beginnings,

And from the World's edge,
To the Styx where I stand,
I guide your soul to
The Ferryman of beginnings.

"And you will realize that
You danced through life,
Just to waltz with me."

42

REVERBERATIONS

Whispers fluttering like
Ethereal wings,
Carrying secrets that
The universe sings.

A delicate ballet,
Words swirl,
Just beyond our grasp,
Like waves kissing shores
With whispered grace,
Only to retreat,
Leaving sands with their trace.

Each syllable, a gemstone
In the cosmic necklace,
A constellation of meaning,
Shimmering bright,
But when we try to hold them,
They dissolve, melting into stardust,
Way beyond the seas, lost to the night.

So we chase after murmur,
Like sailors chasing stars,
Guided by their distant glow,
Their celestial art.

And perhaps
Therein lies the magic—
In the pursuit,
The longing,
The ache of
The heart.

43

UNWRITTEN LETTERS

In the quiet chambers of heart,
  Echoes of longing and regrets depart,
A profound, unspoken conversations lie,
Symphonies of souls transcending time.

Words, hover at speech's door,
Colors stun as the silence roars,
Feathers of memories feel brushing by,
Like a soft tender butterfly.

They are scattered verses of unfinished poems,
Those who never found their inks, letters unwritten,
Promises left hanging in the moon's glow,
And the secrets buried deep within our souls.

Sometimes they shimmer like distant stars,
Other times they weigh cold and heavy as bars,
Becoming a piercing ache when they depart,
And leave scathing marks on the etched hearts.

Yet, they speak volumes in their silence,
Without a sound speak in their absence,
Void echoes with what might have beens,
A bittersweet taste of unvoiced screams.

We bear these, the silence of these words, unspoken
Hold dear their spell, and its power unbroken,
Secrets that ties us to the realms of unseen,
Reminds us that some truths are best kept within.

44

LOVE FORBIDDEN

Ascent, a spark, that ignites a tempest high,
Unveiling a realm where senses lie.
Held captive, a world unseen, unfolds,
Leaving whispers where the story's yet untold.

Your touch, engraved on a forbidden shore,
A yearning, a whisper, that reason can't ignore.

Eyes locked, a secret silently spoken,
A bond blossomed, a promise unbroken.
As shadows lengthen, breaths turn to sigh,
In this trance, a truth we both deny.

Bridge across a chasm, we cannot mend,
A love forbidden, a love that will not end.
Moon, a witness, hangs heavy with despair,
A love so fierce, a love we cannot share.

We dance on embers, passion taking flight,
Knowing the dawn will bring a burning light.

Stolen moments,
A clandestine embrace,
The bitter taste of love,
In a forbidden space.

45

MEMORIES I WILL NEVER HOLD

How you pave the world, at gentle pace,
And tap on earth with newfound grace,

Have you kissed the Sun's fierce flames!
You bear such burning love, untamed.

Like scent of the rising air,
From the rain-kissed earth,
Freeing incense etched in soil,
You paint rains so fragrant,
I fail to remember, its a torrent.

Like emerald blades with sun-soaked hue,
We drenched in warmth, yet suffered too,
When shadows invited us in a chilling maze,
We have been to its depths and ice cold gaze.

Holding corners of the world, forever,
We shared secrets holding hands together,
I love how the night's ink dissolves,

In your sapphire eyes,
As we whisper confessions beneath starlit skies.

Between the worlds, memories stir,
Moments stretch where dreams blur,
The earth sighs, with every breath you take,
A different life, tremor in its wake.

As waxen moon wanes in chilling realms,
We strayed to oceans as broken streams,
We breathed hope and exhaled dreams,
Aching for all, what could have been.

As the daybreak kisses the horizon,
And fragrant dawn arrives,
I am left with all the memories alone,

Kisses bespoken,
Conversations lost,
Dreams unappeased,
Love, left to grow cold.

Memories, I will never have,
Memories, I will never hold.

WHOSE SILENCE ARE YOU

Whose silence are you?
        Where do you wish to be?

Are you the gentle breeze,
Carrying fragrant memories,
Or the air hanging still,
Reminiscing moments it once carried,
Fluttering past distant seas?

Perhaps you are the sun-kissed ivory
Of dandelions,
Cradling the secrets
Within each
Miniature delicate leaf.

Maybe you are the silence
Between day and night,
Where horizon blurs,
And nature holds its breath,
Reluctant to bid farewell
To the Sun and seas.

Could you be the
Secret love notes,
Letter by letter,
Carried by birds
Across the horizon?

And what of the silence
before the tolling bell?
A message spread,
With the sound as it leaves?
As I traverse your silence,
I travel across seven seas.

In this moment, breathless,
Souls merge,
Time stops in this moment - forever,
Between the silence of our beings,
We submerge.

Time is oozing from my pores,
I have waited so patiently,
The moment I quiet my mind,
My soul whispers to you secretly.

Who are you within the
Silence of your thoughts,
Or within the void, meaning to be?

Whose silence are you?
Where do you yearn to be?

ON AND ON

And suddenly it dawned on me
     If you take it
It's yours,
And if you don't, it passes on,
It starts to live when you believe it,
It ceases to exist if you ignore it.

The easiest thing to hurl around
The hardest thing to own
It is always others'
And never one's own.

Nobody wants it,
Everybody places it,
Without beginning,
And without end,
Such is the life of blame.

PROMISES

When you gave me your hand
And entrusted me with it till the end,
When you rested in my arms and
Shared your dreams till word's end,

Was that because you believed in me,
Or because you found solace in me!!

When you whispered those words,
I treasured their ringing touch,
With the promise
To turn each of your words true,
And let your wild thoughts run too.

Was that because you desired me true,
Or because you had rivers running through!!

When I took that hand
I was sure I wanted you, but
I can't do it before I lose myself to you.

I thought I owned your soul
But I didn't, before I lost my own.

How can I give what I don't possess
And now you have the freedom,

I cannot reclaim,
I must confess.

DIVE

O^{h!} You talk so profoundly.

I have always
Been one to wander.

Oh really!
Yes,

Even in this quietude
There is a world
To discover.

Like what!
Well, let's start
With the galaxies
In your eyes,
My Love!!

COFFEE & COCKTAILS

A walk down the memory lane,
        Adorned with the moments we have favored,
And all the times we have treasured,
We celebrate the beautiful companionship,
And the songs we composed together,
Relish all the melodies of friendships.

All the mornings and evenings
We have spent together.
Beaming with laughter & cheer over coffee
Thrilling our way to the cocktail of gossip.

Days will be empty without those times
And flutes of hours will be empty
Without all those wines.

A memory that always excites,
But the vacuum will not subside.

We pray for you that
Memories follow you through,

Even when you are long gone and
Don't want to pass through.

Remember the beautiful times we spent
Will be cherished forever,
The bond we share is strong
And made to last,
We pray it lasts forever.

Saying hi's to new adventures,
As you take a step ahead.
And will say hello to
New coffees and cocktails.

Aarti Bhardwaj, a diverse background of professional lawyer and management graduate turned entrepreneur has shaped author's unique perspective. Her passion for photography has honed her ability to capture moments and emotions, which often finds its way into her prose.

A dedicated reading enthusiast, Aarti Bhardwaj has immersed herself in various genres, expanding her knowledge and enriching her storytelling abilities. Through writing Aarti Bhardwaj seeks to explore the complexities of human nature and the interconnectedness of our world. The work often delves into themes of personal growth, and the power of resilience. With a touch of vulnerability and a hint of reality she invite readers to embark on a journey of self-discovery and reflection.

Made in the USA
Monee, IL
07 July 2026

56552213R00069